THE SECRETS TO MANAGING A

HIGH-PERFORMING HEALTH CENTER

BASED ON THE SUCCESS PRINCIPLES OF NAPOLEON HILL

By David L. Brown

Health Center Board President

THE SECRETS TO MANAGING A

HIGH-PERFORMING HEALTH CENTER

BASED ON THE SUCCESS PRINCIPLES OF NAPOLEON HILL

By David L. Brown

Health Center Board President

Cover creator: Brad Szollose
brad@liquidleadership.com

Cover photo credit: Sutterstock

Group of business people; Image ID: 60460822 By Kurhan

Smiling female doctors and nurses with stethoscope; Image ID: 255041803 By Syda Productions

Table of Contents

Acknowledgement

To my fantastic wife, Debbie, who is always there with encouragement, support and the occasional kick in the pants. Thank you for being there.

With all my love
Dave

Dedication

This book is dedicated to all the hard workingmen and women who have dedicated their lives to improving the health of their communities. In the community health center movement countless people have volunteered to lead the organizations to success.

To all who are involved I say to you, "God Bless You". I am deeply honored to be part of this program doing so much with so little.

Keep up the great work you are doing.

Foreword

Because I have been hospitalized about 40 times, have had 4 hips, 4 knees and 2 shoulders replaced, and received hundreds of home visits from various healthcare providers, I am very familiar with the many benefits a good healthcare system provides.

I am also the world's most well known Napoleon Hill Foundation Certified Instructor. The 17 Principles of Success taught by the Napoleon Hill Foundation and myself contain the wisdom and experience of some of the most well-known and accomplished people in the history of the United States, and are based on the 25 years of research that Napoleon Hill invested learning firsthand from them.

Napoleon Hill's book, *Think and Grow Rich*, is one of the top 10-bestselling non-fiction books of all time. It has sold over 100 million copies in various formats and has been translated into many languages.

My website attracts visitors from more than 135 countries every month, proof that Napoleon Hill is searched for and admired around the world.

My AMAZING friend David Brown is both an avid follower of Napoleon Hill and his proven success principles and a devoted and dedicated health center Board member. The challenges he writes about are real and the solutions he suggests are necessary to continue to deliver the highest quality healthcare services, efficiently and effectively, to the people you serve.

I urge you to engage with David and mastermind with him to help your health center, and all health centers, be an asset and blessing in your community and across the United States. By following the ideas in this book, and masterminding with David, you will be proactive about the challenges your Board faces, and be able to plan ahead, rather than being reactive to changes and circumstances.

You are a huge part of the future success of the United States. Be a positive, determined and creative part of the healthcare solutions your community and country need in the coming years. People are depending on you.

Pursue your Purpose with Passion to make this world a better place to live.

Tom too tall Cunningham
Napoleon Hill Foundation Certified Instructor
Creator of the Journeys To Success book series
Founder and Host of Journey To Success Radio
International Inspirational Speaker

Testimonials

"I must admit prior to reading this I was not familiar with Napoleon Hill but now you've introduced us so I will be trolling Amazon Books tonight looking for his work.

You have written from the eyes of a Consumer Board Member but one might assume the same "17 Success Principles" could easily be applied to CHC CEOs and their C-Suites. Thank you for sharing your "AH HA" moment, your thoughts and subsequent research. A valuable read for all of us as we navigate these uncertain days ahead."

—Anita Monoian
Health Center, CEO

"David has done a good job of applying the principles he has found in his study of the works of Napoleon Hill to his experience as a Board Member of a Federally Qualified Health Center (FQHC).

Because the work of FQHC's is unique in the many locations across the USA, and it's Governing Board Members truly represent the community, applying these principles is a great exercise in personal and corporate self-discovery. Serving on a FQHC Board is unique and it needs to be approached with purpose and intentional effort.

Heading into my 31st year as a FQHC Board Member, with lots of leadership service experience in Local, State and National Organizations, I found the opportunity to review my own application of David's thoughts, and found it an enjoyable journey."

—John Price
Health Center Board, Chair

"This book is superb! This is a must read manual for every board member for all health Center board members. It keeps you focused and positive. I wish I had it 37 years ago. What a treasure."

—Pam LaPan
Health Center Board, Past President

"As I read your book, I kept thinking; 'my board members would appreciate the principles as well as the lessons'. Of course, all our staff would also benefit! While some of the lessons are "common sense", occasionally we must be reminded. This book will help readers focus on doing the right thing for their Health Center. Thanks for your work on this, David, well done!"

—Rachel A. Gonzales
Hanson, CEO

"Having had the pleasure of knowing Mr. David Brown through our health center work over the last several years, I am thrilled to see him write this book!! One of the distinguishing pillars of a successful Community Health Center is the Board Governance structure that allows each community to have a say in the healthcare that is delivered within the community. This book does a fantastic job of relating how Boards can benefit from strong business ethics, ideas, and leadership and helps to bridge the gap from the ideological concept of governance to the actual hands on practices that Boards need to help them be successful. As always Dave, way to lead by example!! Thanks for writing this book!!"

—Ellen Adlam
Peninsula Community Health Centers of Alaska, Board Member
Alaska Primary Care Association Consumer, Board Representative

Preface

Why this book?

Health centers have been growing and will continue to grow to fill a need in healthcare. Not only are they growing in the number of organizations and delivery sites but in the size of the organizations. The growth in size often comes with a growth in complexity.

The funding levels spurring growth also bring the spotlight focused on the movement. There are more calls for transparency and making sure those in authority positions of health centers are being good stewards of the funds. This is why we see the site visits conducted and boards being held accountable.

With over thirteen hundred health center organizations across the country you will find many different levels of success. One reason is where the organizations are in the life cycles. Another part is based on the workings of the board and their ability to perform their required duties. Bad choices can cause a center to have declining revenues leading to defunding or merger with other organizations.

As I am writing this, we are first 100 days of a new president. This could lead to additional pressure and questions. It would be nice if we could look into a crystal ball for guidance, but that only works in fairy tales. Will the next administration be as supportive as the prior ones? We don't know, but we do know that health center advocates telling their story alongside the work of the National Association of Community Health Centers (NACHC) will continue to be important to maintain bipartisan support health centers have enjoyed for their more than 50 year history.

There are many discussions going on as to what will change under our new President around the Affordable Care Act (ACA). Part of this act was Medicaid expansion and various funding opportunities. Should state Medicaid funding be changed to block grants and/or Medicaid expansion be eliminated there will be some tough decisions to be made to ensure the continued financial viability of health center organizations.

The growth health centers have accomplished forces us to change the way we think. For many years we were Mom & Pop type of business; now we are large multimillion-dollar corporations. My board Treasurer keeps reminding us of this and to think like the organizations we have become.

Being a health center board member I also have a day job. A part of my day job is an author. When I was writing a chapter for my last book, "Journeys to success, 21 empowering stories based on the success principles of Napoleon Hill," I had an AH HA moment. Reviewing these principles, it hit me like a brick these same principles not only affect my personal life but that applying these to the health center board as a whole contributes to our success.

This revelation made me examine some of the health centers both successful and not as successful. What makes some centers successful while others don't reach that level? My findings were that those that do not reach high levels of success are not applying the success principles.

We as a health center movement are only as successful as the weakest center. That's why; I felt that this information needed to be shared. My goal for this book is it that it serves as another tool assisting to raise all health centers to high levels of success.

Throughout the pages you will find discussion on these principles, their meaning and how they can be applied to our work as boards of directors. You can also think about how they apply to you as an individual and your life in and out of the health center movement.

Thank you for taking time to read and digest this material. Put it to work for you and your center. Share it with other board members. Together we can improve the levels of success experienced health centers across the nation.

Have questions email me at:

david@dbrowncompany.com

David L. Brown

CHAPTER 1

My Discovery of Napoleon Hill

*"If you do not conquer self,
you will be conquered by self."*

— Napoleon Hill

L et me set the stage I was working in a factory and a strike was looming on the horizon. I was thinking to myself that I needed to find something new, that I didn't want to go back to the factory.

Scanning the classified ads, there was a sales position ad for a prominent insurance company. I responded to the ad and the interview was scheduled. Following the interview there was a several month process you had to go through before an offer would be made.

Before signing on the dotted line to become an agent, you had to obtain state insurance licenses. This required a self-study course and you a two-week in-person course. Completion of these there was followed by another two week company training. These were only offered a few times per year therefore, there was a time gap between completing the pre-requisite training and the company training.

During this time the recruiter gave me a book. I had not had heard of it or the author before. The book was *Think and Grow Rich* by Napoleon Hill. The recruiter told me to read and study this book and apply the principles within. This was my introduction to Napoleon Hill.

Converting from factory worker mindset living for payday and days off to business owner took effort and time. Until this point personal development was not on my radar screen. The new career brought this to my attention. Reading self-help and sales training books became a way of life for me.

My Discovery of Napoleon Hill

This was over 30 years ago and life and circumstances have changed. Becoming an author has provided me the opportunity to meet others who are in the self-development field as authors and speakers. The one author and book that keeps coming up the most is Napoleon Hill and *Think and Grow Rich*.

Hill had written many books and I have read several of them over and over. I always pick up something new each time I read them. *Think and Grow Rich* has become an annual read for me. There is so much to learn from Hill and his works. The copy originally given to me has been read so much the cover had to be taped together, pages are yellowed and some ink has begun coming off the paper.

I want to encourage you to go out and get yourself a copy of this amazing book. Consider this your introduction to Napoleon Hill. May you become as good a friend with him as I have!

CHAPTER 2

Who is Napoleon Hill?

"More gold had been mined
from the mind of men
than the earth itself"

— Napoleon Hill

N apoleon Hill wrote *Think and Grow Rich* in 1937. There is much more to the man than that. Let me tell you about how *Think and Grow Rich* came to be and more about Hill.

Napoleon was working for a coalmine company when it closed. In order to meet his purpose in life he took a position writing for Bob Taylor's Magazine in 1908. His agreement in writing for the magazine was to exclusively profile giants of industry and business.

His first interview was with Andrew Carnegie. This is where his life would forever change. As Hill listened to Carnegie describe his journey from poverty to wealth, he could personally feel the impact and Carnegie sensed the influence he was having leading Carnegie to invite Hill to spend the weekend with him and continue their discussion. Hill had no idea that this conversation would become the basis of his work and that would it lead to his fame thirty years in the future.

In his conversation with Carnegie, Hill learned of other great leaders who had similar backgrounds. These included people like Ford, Edison, Rockefeller Firestone and Alexander Graham Bell. They all learned their lessons by trial and error. Carnegie believed that anyone could improve their situation by studying leaders such as these and others.

During this weekend visit, Carnegie described a project that required extensive interviews with hundreds of leaders from all walks of life along with studying those great leaders that had passed on. Once the interviews were done defining a comprehensive set of principles that these leaders applied would not be easy. Carnegie estimated this type of project would require at least twenty years.

After Carnegie described the project he envisioned he offered it to Hill. Having a similar belief as Carnegie, Hill accepted the opportunity in seconds. The next part caught Hill off guard. During this twenty-year period he would have to earn his own way, as there would be no pay other than reimbursement of his out-of-pocket expenses. Carnegie would provide him with letters of introduction to the leaders he would interview.

Over the next twenty years Hill would rise to fame and fortune only to lose it all. This cycle would repeat itself many times. Each time, Hill's definiteness of purpose would enable him to get up and do it again.

Some of the things he did over this time were to write for various publications, publish his own magazine, consult with businesses and even become an advisor to presidents.

To learn more about Napoleon Hill and his journey read the book *A Lifetime of Riches* by Michael J. Ritt Jr. and Kirk Landers. You can also visit the Napoleon Hill Foundation website at www.naphill.org. That is where I found this partial timeline of Hill's achievements.

- **1883 Born in Wise County, Virginia**
- **1908 Andrew Carnegie induces him to organize**

the world's first philosophy of personal achievement

- 1919 Publishes Hill's *Golden Rules Magazine*
- 1921-1923 Publishes *Napoleon Hill's Magazine*
- 1928 Publishes *Law of Success*
- 1930 Publishes *The Magic Ladder to Success*
- 1933-36 Presidential Advisor to President Franklin D. Roosevelt
- 1937 Publishes *Think & Grow Rich*
- 1939 Publishes *How to Sell Your Way Through Life*
- 1941 Publishes *Mental Dynamite* study course in 17 volumes
- 1942 Mental Dynamite program discontinued with advent of World War II
- 1945 Publishes *The Master Key to Riches*
- 1952 -62 Associates with W. Clement Stone of Combined Insurance Co. of America. Teaches his Philosophy of Personal Achievement. Lectures on *"Science of Success"*
- 1953 Publishes *How to Raise Your Own Salary*
- 1959 Publishes *Success Through a Positive Mental Attitude*

- **1961 Publishes** *PMA: Science of Success* **Course**
- **1967 Publishes** *Grow Rich with Peace of Mind*
- **1970 Publishes** *Succeed and Grow Rich Through Persuasion*
- **Passes away in November**

The principles Hill discovered and published in Think and Grow Rich have sold over one hundred million copies to date. These principles not only apply to individuals, but are also easily applied to groups and even companies.

As I explained in the preface successful health centers are applying these principles and don't realize, I certainly didn't. That is the reason for the AH HA moment.

The remainder of this book discusses the 17 Success Principles and how they apply to our work as health centerboards.

CHAPTER 3

Success Principles

"The starting point of all achievement is DESIRE. Keep this constantly in mind. Weak desire brings weak results, just as a small fire makes a small amount of heat."

— Napoleon Hill

*I*n the preface I shared my AH HA moment with you and how it led me to this book. What are these principles I keep talking about? Where did they come from? Who is Napoleon Hill? Here is the story.

Over the twenty years Hill spent interviewing the rags-to-riches tycoons he analyzed them to a series of 17 success principles. These principles are well over a hundred years old but are still as relevant today as they were they day they were discovered.

In the following pages we will break each principle into a description of the meaning and how it applies to our work as aboard and board member.

Here is a list of the principles:

1. Definiteness of Purpose
2. Mastermind Alliance
3. Applied Faith
4. Going the Extra Mile
5. Pleasing Personality
6. Personal Initiative
7. Positive Mental Attitude
8. Enthusiasm
9. Self-Discipline
10. Accurate Thinking
11. Controlled Attention
12. Teamwork
13. Learning from Adversity and Defeat
14. Creative Vision
15. Maintenance of Sound Health
16. Budgeting Time and Money
17. Cosmic Habitforce

As you read through the list of principles did any jump out? Look at these from the standpoint of a health centerboard, as a whole would apply them while completing their work. We will look at each of these principles and how they apply to the board. Think about how you as a person can apply these to your life and your work on the board. Consider this a personal development exercise, which we all need to do. When we improve ourselves we improve the outcomes of what we do.

1) Definiteness of Purpose

Hill describes this as the starting point for all achievement. Without purpose and a plan, people drift aimlessly through life. Successful people move on their own initiative but they know where they are going before they start.

Hill is known for the saying *"Whatever the mind of man can conceive and believe it can achieve."*

As health center board members, we have to have a burning desire to be successful. Individual board members must believe we can make a difference in the communities we serve. That desire extends to our individual desire to participate to the fullest by attending committee and board meetings.

Applying the definiteness of purpose principle to the board as a whole, our purpose is written in our organizational mission statement. After all, don't we exist to provide high quality, cost effective care to all regardless of their ability to pay?

Our mission should be front and center in our minds as we make decisions. Whether expanding services, adding or changing a location or adding staff, we must ask ourselves, "How does this further or enhance the mission and serve our patients?

Strengthen your purpose by picturing a successful organization in your mind. See it – Believe it - Achieve it.

2) Mastermind Alliance

Hill defines power through the mastermind as: coordination of knowledge and effort, in a spirit of harmony between two or more people for the attainment of a definite purpose.

In 1965 when Doctors Geiger and Gibson began the health center movement, the board was a critical component of the success of a health center. Their research indicated that if you give communities a say in how their health care is delivered they will find a way and it will be successful. A patient majority board gives that say in how care is delivered.

The Federal Health Center Program requirements also state that board members should have various backgrounds sufficient enough to serve the organization and their work. Some examples are, but not limited to: finance, legal, business, social programs, government and health. These backgrounds also form a good foundation for a mastermind alliance.

One thing not mentioned in the regulations is that board members must believe in the mission (definiteness of purpose) and work harmoniously with one another. As a board chair myself, I certainly would not want a board member who wasn't supportive of the mission or didn't want to play in the same sandbox.

You can see how the board does constitute a true mastermind group. Use it wisely. The energy created from this meeting of the minds becomes available to each individual person in the group.

3) Applied Faith

Hill defines this as: a state of mind, which may develop by conditioning your mind to receive Infinite Intelligence. Applied faith is the adapting of the Infinite Intelligence to a definite major purpose.

There are many things we need to have faith in as board members. My faith in health centers and the mission began over thirty years ago. I was asked to by our township supervisor to represent the township on a medical board. I told him I would take a look and let him know.

After contacting the health center, sitting through a board meeting, and learning about the mission, I was hooked. The passion the members had for the mission touched my heartstrings and, over thirty years later, I am still there.

One of the charges to the board is hire the CEO. We must have faith in this individual to effectively run the day-to-day operation and hire qualified passionate staff.

Faith in ourselves as a group and individually that we can and do make a difference in the lives of our patients is critical. This passion truly does make a difference when we speak to legislators. Board members have no other reason to speak so loudly about health centers other than our faith in the movement and the mission.

By using the faith in our hearts and our minds, we can make a difference in the lives of our patients and the communities we serve. Improving access to care and reducing health disparities are part of the reason we exist. Without the faith and intelligence to believe we can make a difference, we would not be here.

4) Going the Extra Mile

Hill describes this as giving more and better service than you are paid for and sooner or later you will receive compound interest on compound interest from your investment. He goes on to say "The most successful people are those that serve the greatest number of people."

Boards of directors have several ways we go above and beyond the call of duty. One is for all of our patients and another is for our staff.

Patients are the reason we exist. Our desire is to provide high quality care to them as well as appropriate services to improve their access to care. This means that after doing our due diligence, sometimes it's a leap of faith we take to add service or location if we feel it can be supported.

Staff allows us to do what we do. Without them providing the care, we wouldn't exist. I encourage every board member while sitting in the waiting room to pay attention to the interaction between staff and patients. Compliment if it is warranted; you would be surprised how much that means to them. I have always said that I am the first to complain, but I am also always first to compliment. Make sure you share with the CEO good and bad.

Recently I was sitting in the waiting room waiting to see my provider and just observing. The receptionist was working with a patient and as I watched how she dealt with them was amazing. She actually made the patient feel at ease, helping her to a comfortable seat and getting her a drink of water while she waited for her to take care of the issue. Seeing the face of the patient told the story. I had to compliment the receptionist on her caring attitude and how she handled everything. When I got home, off went an email to the CEO explaining what I observed so he, too, knew what happened.

Another way our board went the extra mile is through the benefits we offer to our staff. With the ever-increasing cost of benefits as a board were forced to make tough decisions to reduce the increase in cost. Being creative and working with our benefit broker, we devised a way to not only save money, but also keep staff whole when we increased the deductible on the health plan.

Surprise the staff with a bonus or even a catered meal as an appreciation from the board. Celebrate the victories they accomplish, such as positive operational site visit or Joint Commission accreditation.

Staff has to pay a portion of the cost of the health care plan and they were happy to find out their cost would stay the same. When the broker explained the high deductible plan and the Health Savings Plan we funded so they would not see the increase out of pocket they were extremely happy.

5) Pleasing Personality

Hill describes a pleasing personality as the combination of all the agreeable, gratifying and likeable qualities of any one individual. He goes on to say "It is essential that you develop a pleasing personality – pleasing to yourself and others."

Every person you come in contact with deserves to be greeted with a pleasing personality. Being grouchy usually makes the doors in peoples mind close to new ideas and creates negativity. Nothing positive will happen this way. A pleasant personality will have the opposite effect. People will want to be around you and will be more open to listening to your thoughts and ideas. When you feel pleasant and believe in yourself, good things happen.

Board members are ambassadors in the community for the center. They also meet with potential partners, funders or collaborative agencies. We want to leave pleasing and positive impression.

I know you are saying this is common sense but it still needs saying. Check your negative attitude and grumpiness at the door.

A pleasing personality also makes you feel better mentally and physically. People will want to be around you. You will want to do things. Stay upbeat and share your happiness with those near you. You will make a difference.

6) Personal Initiative

Hill says personal initiative bears the same relationship to an individual that a self-starter bears to an automobile! It is the power that starts all action. It is the power that assures completion of anything one begins. Personal initiative is self-motivation.

A commitment to participation, progress and meeting goals is required to be a board member for a health center. We agree to become part of the organization and motivate ourselves to participate to the fullest extent possible. Yes we are volunteers and have a day job, but that is no excuse to not show up at meetings and participate.

Volunteer for ad hoc committees of the board. Or maybe there is a project you want to bring to the board, do your homework first before bringing it forward. Take initiative to help recruit board members to fill openings, always keep your ears open. After all, we are in the community.

Take it upon yourself to become involved not just at your health center but also at the primary care association and at the National Association of Community Health Centers (NACHC). There are many ways to get involved; committee membership is a good way to start to get familiar. You could run for a board position. Attend conferences where you can learn and meet other board members from around the state and country.

7) Positive Mental Attitude

Hill says your mental attitude is the medium by which you can balance your life and your relationship to people and circumstances – to attract what you desire.

We are all born equal, in the sense that we all have equal access to the Great Principle: the right to control our thoughts and mental attitude. A positive mental attitude is the greatest of life's riches...it is through the attitude that anything worthwhile is achieved.

Keep your mind on the things you want and off the things you don't want. Remember the old proverb: "Be careful what you set your heart on, for you will surely achieve it."

The choice of being positive or negative is up to you. Much more can be accomplished being positive than in being a "Negative Nellie." As with the pleasing personality you feel better with a positive attitude both mentally and physically.

Attitudes are contagious. Your attitude can spread to those around you and/or drive them away.

What type of people are you surrounded by? Distance yourself from those with a negative attitude if possible.

When it's time for committee or board meetings if you have the negative attitude, make sure you check it at the door. Not much will be accomplished if part of the group has a negative attitude.

8) Enthusiasm

Hill describes enthusiasm as faith in action. Saying; "It inspires action and it is the most contagious of all emotions." He goes on to describe enthusiasm as a combination of mental and physical energy "To be enthusiastic – act enthusiastically!"

Applying this to ourselves and as board members we need to take on assignments and actions willingly and ready to fulfill them to the best of your ability.

Some examples of enthusiasm in action may be volunteering for a committee to learn more about the workings in a health center from a different way. How about running for an officer position? This is a great way to get involved at a deeper level and learn. A pearl of wisdom my Dad passed along to me was, "If you want to know how the organization runs, get on the executive committee."

Our work as a board member is exciting and fulfilling. That for me is enough to be enthusiastic all by itself. Like a positive mental attitude, enthusiasm is contagious. When we tell our story to legislators and policy makers we need to tell it with enthusiasm. It will show the passion we have for what we do as health centers. This has never been more important than it is in today's political climate.

9) Self-Discipline

Hill says self-discipline, or self-control, means taking possession of your own mind.

The power of thought is the only thing over which any human has complete and unquestionable control. We have the power of self-determination, the ability to choose what our thoughts and actions will be. If you direct your thoughts and control your emotions, you will define your destiny. Take charge of your life. You are what you think.

A good example is reading your board packet. One of the duties of a board member is to come to the meetings prepared. The last thing you want to hear is someone ripping open the envelope for the first time in the board meeting.

Attending board and committee meetings is a commitment we accept. It takes self-discipline to attend as many as possible. We all have scheduling conflicts and it's up to each of us to minimize the number of them.

Self-discipline affects all aspects of our lives. There is always something else we could be doing instead of going to a meeting, or attending a function. We must force ourselves to do what we have committed to.

Your self-discipline begins by mastering your thoughts. Not controlling your thoughts leads to not controlling your deeds. It calls for balancing your emotions in your heart with the reasoning in your head.

10) Accurate Thinking

Hill states accurate thought involves two fundamentals. First, you must separate facts from mere information. Second, you must separate facts into two classes – the important and the unimportant. Only by doing this can you think clearly and accurately.

Accurate thinkers permit no one to do their thinking for them. Gather information and listen to others opinions, but reserve for you the decision-making. "Truth will be truth, regardless of a closed mind, ignorance, or the refusal to believe," says Hill.

We make critical decisions on a regular basis at board meetings. In order to make the correct decisions, we must understand why accurate thinking is so vital to the success of the health center. This includes doing our due diligence to make sure the questions we ask will allow us to make the best decisions possible.

Part of being an accurate thinker is to not let anyone think for us. Our job is to gather the necessary information, listen to the opinions of others, and exercise the privilege of making an informed decision.

11) Controlled Attention

Hill defines controlled attention as the act of coordinating all the faculties of our mind and directing their combined power to a given end. It is the act, which can be achieved only by the strictest sort of self-discipline.

Another way to describe controlled attention is coordinating our entire mind in directing that power to a given end. This is a matter of a strict type of self-discipline.

Learning to fix our undivided attention to any given object for a length of time, we will have learned the power of concentration. We need to keep our minds focused on what we want and off the things we don't. You become what you think about the most.

You could also describe this as focus, paying attention to the information and discussion being presented on a given topic. There is a lot of information being presented at meetings and by letting our minds drift we may miss a key piece of information that could lead us to take an incorrect action.

12) Teamwork

Hill describes teamwork as harmonious cooperation that is willing, voluntary and free. Whenever the spirit of teamwork is the dominating influence in business or inventory, success is inevitable. Harmonious cooperation is a priceless asset that you can acquire in proportion to your giving.

Teamwork is not the same as the mastermind principle. Teamwork is working together without necessarily having definiteness of purpose.

Our work on the board is all about teamwork and the mastermind principle. We must all come together to get the job done. As we take action it doesn't mean we all have to agree one hundred percent. We can agree to disagree with a topic, make sure it is done respectfully. Then when we walk out of the room we the support the majority, regardless of how we felt about the issue.

For example, you have a group of board members who want to control the action of the board and have an ulterior motive. They intimidate the other board members. The controlling group by taking action on their hidden agenda ends up putting the entire organization at risk.

Teamwork needs to be encouraged and carried out. The board leads by example. Look at successful centers and you will see this in action.

13) Learning From Adversity and Defeat

Hill teaches that; every adversity you meet carries with it a seed of equivalent or greater benefit. Realize this statement and believe in it. Close the door of your mind on all the failures and circumstances of your past so your mind can operate in a Positive Mental Attitude. Every problem has a solution –only you have to find it.

If you develop an "I don't believe in defeat" attitude, you will learn there is no such thing as defeat – unless you accept it. If you can look at the problem as a temporary setback and a stepping-stone to success, you will come to believe that the only limitations you have are in your own mind.

So-called failures represent only a temporary defeat. Sometimes they can be a blessing in disguise. How can I say that?

Think about a time in your life when something didn't go as planned and you had to stop and evaluate what happened. Or something did not get approved and, all of a sudden, a new opportunity presented itself that was even more advantageous than what you tried.

Think back to action the board took that did not go as planned. This could be a grant application that was denied or an expansion didn't work out. What about hiring a CEO? Many years ago we had to hire a new CEO. A procedure was in place as to how it would be done: detailed qualifications; interview process explained; and committee make up to handle the process. Ads were placed and the resumes began coming in. They were narrowed down to potential interview candidates. The board through their process picked a candidate to offer a contract the individual was invited to meet the management team and learn more about the operation.

During this process I had taken a leave of absence from the board to fill the role of Interim CEO. After the candidate met with the management team one on one it felt like a revolving door in my office. Each had concerns from their meetings. The board was to hear discussion on the candidate before making the contract offer. During my time, I had each management team member spill their guts. The board did not offer the contract.

Now what? A post-mortem discussion took place. We dissected what happened and felt it was the pool of candidates versus our process. It was decided to repeat our process. This time around, we hired such an excellent CEO that as a board still pat ourselves on the back for our decision.

No matter what the challenge, we can always learn from it. It is only a permanent defeat when we quit or give up. If you aren't happy with the direction things are going, don't be afraid to stop, analyze, adjust and act.

How do you know if something isn't going right? If we are monitoring the activity of the center as we are supposed to do, we can possibly spot things that aren't going as planned. Don't be afraid to ask questions and never stop learning.

14) Creative Vision

Hill's belief that creative vision is a quality of mind belonging to men and women who follow the habit of going the extra mile, it doesn't recognize the concept of regular working hours is not concerned with the monetary pay, and its highest aim is to do the impossible.

Creative vision is closely related to the state of mind known as faith, and it is significant that those who have demonstrated the most creative vision are those known to have the greatest capacity for faith.

One of the sayings I've heard over and over again during my involvement is, "We need to think out of the box!" We have to be fearless in the use of our imagination.

When we crafted our mission and vision for our centers, we tapped into that creative vision. Do you think Doctors Geiger and Gibson tapped into their creative vision when they designed the health center model back in 1965?

Health centers have always been creative on how things are done. One reason is that we don't have the pockets as deep as the large health systems. We have always found a way to do more with less.

Having a volunteer board of directors with a patient majority is creative all by itself. This unique board model naturally brings with it a great deal of creativity. This is a true example of the mastermind principle working in health centers.

Creativity really shows up in strategic planning processes. Ideas flow out during the brainstorming, and then we get creative on how to implement them. The definiteness of purpose - our desire to improve access, reduce disparities and improve the health of communities provides us the motivation to put our thinking caps on.

"The imagination is the workshop of the soul wherein are shaped all plans for individual achievement."

— Napoleon Hill

15) Maintenance of Sound Health

Hill tells us to follow work with play, mental effort with physical, eating with fasting, seriousness with humor, and you will be on the road to sound health and happiness. Don't try and cure a headache but rather the thing that causes the headache. Whatever you possess, material, mental, or spiritual you must use it or lose it.

You are a mind with a body! Your brain controls the body; know that sound physical health is dependent on a positive mental attitude. Establish sound, well-balanced health habits in work, play, rest, nourishment and study. Develop and maintain positive thought habits. Remember that what your mind focuses upon, your mind brings into existence. "If you think you're sick, you are."

It's not easy and takes discipline both mental and physical. We must maintain our personal health to fulfill our duty on the board. When we feel good our energy level is higher and our brain seems to work better allowing us to contribute effectively to discussions.

Applying the sound health principle to the center is also a must. What makes a health center have sound health? This is subject to interpretation of each organization. Common items include solid finances, money in the bank or a positive balance sheet. Warning, Will Robinson, Warning!!! You can have a positive balance sheet and still have cash flow issues. You must make the decision as a board.

How do we know if we are in good financial shape? Everyone MUST know what is required to be reviewed on a monthly basis. HRSA details this information in the site visit guide. Comparing actual to monthly and year to date and budget will provide data. If you are looking at this regularly, you can see if your revenue is going up or down. Keep in mind that everything we do at this time is encounter based.

If the health of the organization begins to deteriorate, the board must be prepared to ask questions and take action if necessary. This may mean making hard and unpopular decisions.

Boards are held responsible for the success of health centers. We must use due diligence to carry out this duty and maintain a healthy organization.

16) Budgeting Time and Money

Hill teaches in this principle that the effectiveness in human endeavor calls for the organized budget of time. For the average person, the 24 hours of each day should be divided as follows: 8 hours for sleep, 8 hours for work, 8 hours for recreation and spare time.

The successful person budgets time, income, and expenditures, living within their means. The failure squanders time and income with a disregard for their value. Hill says, "Tell me how you spend your spare time and how you spend your money, and I will tell you where and what you will be ten years from now."

We all know about budgeting money and why it's important. We are required to submit and approve an annual budget for the health center besides it's a good business practice.

It is very important that the board understand how the budget is created and what assumptions are being used. Currently our payments are based on encounters. This most likely will be changing in the future. The finance committee should review the budget and then it is presented to the full board for review and approval.

Budgeting time is a completely different story. Most people do not budget their time effectively and we as boards sometime are no different. On the personal side we must budget our time to meet our commitment to fulfill the duties of a board member which includes attending board meetings and meetings of committee you are on. Your attendance is depended on to meet quorum requirements and to provide input.

Budgeting adequate time for board and committee meetings is crucial to getting the work done. In addition to the time for the meetings, we need to be aware staff time for staff that attends the meetings. The CEO is an ex-officio member of the board; time needs to be cleared on their schedule. The same is true for the CFO and the Medical Director and any others. Taking a provider off the patient schedule means they are not generating paid encounters and the board needs to be aware of it.

Effectively using time is a must to stay in compliance with the monthly meeting requirement. If there is an hour planned for the board meeting and it takes two, we did not do a good job on budgeting time. How do we assure that we are budgeting time correctly? A strong board chair is needed to keep the meeting moving and on target.

Volumes have been written on effective leadership so we won't get into that here. One statement I will make is that successful health centers have strong and effective leadership throughout the organization.

The board needs to be frugal when it comes to budgeting both time and money. I have had health center clients whose board meetings last two or three hours. When seeing these, the question I have to ask is, are you using the committee structure effectively? Chances are they are not.

Committees are designed to do the heavy lifting. There are charges for each committee and what they are responsible for - is it being fulfilled? For instance, the personnel committee should be reviewing the employee benefits, salary ranges and personnel policies and then recommending approval once they are satisfied with the outcome. Each committee should be fulfilling their charge.

Depending on the committee meeting agenda the length need to be set aside will vary. It is much easier to work with three to five people than fifteen on the board for example.

You have a budget, but then what do we do next? The finance committee should be reviewing monthly the actual income and expense to budget and to same period last year. This is how you spot financial issues affecting the center. The board treasurer presents a financial report to the board and a recommendation from the finance committee for approval.

Use your committees and you will save time at the board meetings. Board size and composition might make managing the time effectively difficult, but not impossible.

17) Cosmic Habitforce

Hill describes it this way: the orderliness of the world of natural law gives evidence that they are under the control of a universal plan.

Man is the only living creature equipped with the power of choice through which he may establish his own thought and behavior patterns. You have the power to break bad habits and to create good ones in their place–at will. "You are where you are and what you are because of your established habits and thoughts and deeds."

Think about these statements; How do they apply to you as a person? How do you as an individual fit into the overall mix of a health centerboard? Are you bringing to the table any habits that need changing?

Being a board member is not a fit for everyone. Do you have the willpower and drive to help the center reach the level of success desired as a board and organization? Take a deep look inside yourself for an answer. Health centerboards need those who have the drive and inspiration to make a difference.

For any organization I belong to I ask, "Do I truly believe in the mission and have the desire to dedicate the needed time to do my part?" If not, a letter of resignation is submitted. It's not fair to others not to do my share.

You may feel that the centerboard is more than you commit to at the present time. It doesn't mean you should just walk away if you have the passion, but not the time. Is there another place you can be involved without the time commitment, such as an advisory group?

In conclusion

These 17 success principles are found in successful business leaders and businesses. In the beginning of this chapter we said to think of the board as a single person and apply the principles. You understand how they come into play; we may not even realize we are following them. I sure didn't until my AH HA moment described earlier.

[1] Hill's teachings are taken from the Napoleon Hill scrolls. Downloaded from www.tom2tall.com

CHAPTER 4

Summary

"TELL THE WORLD WHAT YOU
INTEND TO DO,
BUT FIRST SHOW IT.
This is the equivalent of saying 'deeds,
and not words, are what count most."

— Napoleon Hill

*L*ook around the country at health centers and you will see they operate at many different levels of success. Some are losing their operating grants, some are being merged into other organizations and some are just disappearing with a new organization taking their place. When this happens the loser is the patients and the communities.

Throughout this book, I mentioned many time that the board is the ultimate responsible party for the success of the health center. How we become successful is about the choices we make and the way we make them. Different boards have different beliefs. This translates into the work they do.

Over my tenure in the health center movement, there have been boards that felt no need for additional training. Therefore, they never attend the state and national meetings. Let me restate that. They do not attend and participate in the workshops and networking events. There are those board members who ask where is it being held? It becomes a paid vacation for them, the center paying the hotel and transportation and they go and never participate. We can no longer allow this to happen. There is too much at stake.

Often we see pride get in the way of asking for help. The fear of looking foolish is in each of us. If your board needs assistance in an area, swallow your pride and ask for help. Your state primary care association, NACHC and the Bureau of Primary Care has help available.

Summary

Look at the successful centers near you and ask them for guidance. Are they doing something that you can S&D (swipe and deploy) for your use?

In closing, here are a few more words of wisdom from Napoleon Hill: "You are where you are and what you are because of your established habits and thoughts and deeds."

If you don't like where you center is on the scale of success, you have the power to change it.

Resources

National Association of Community Health Centers

www.nachc.org

State primary care associations

https://bphc.hrsa.gov/qualityimprovement/strate gicpartnerships/ncapca/associations.html

Bureau of Primary care

https://bphc.hrsa.gov

Napoleon Hill Foundation

http://naphill.org

Recommended reading:

Think and Grow Rich – Napoleon Hill

Laws of Success – Napoleon Hill

Outwitting the Devil – Napoleon Hill

Liquid Leadership, From Woodstock to Wikipedia – Brad Szollose

Journeys to Success series – Tom Cunningham (feel free to read my chapter in *Journeys to Success* volume 1; chapter 11)

Program Requirements – HRSA

Site visit guide – HRSA

Suggestions:

> ➤ Sign up for newsletter from pertinent organizations

> ➤ Follow PCAs, NACHC and other health centers on social media

> ➤ Get involved at the state and national level, get on committees, participate and attend conferences

> ➤ Seek out learning opportunities

About the Author

David is a leader in the health center community. His message is designed to help board members understand their roles and responsibilities and strengthen their knowledge to support the health center and CEO. He is an in-demand speaker and consultant who has helped many health center boards increase their awareness of the demands required of them by HRSA. Sharing his 30 years of experience as a health center board member, he provides real life examples demonstrating the application of the rules.

His commitment has led him to serve as the Chair of his health center board for over 20 years. He became the first health center board member to serve as President of Michigan Primary Care Association

(MPCA), serving 2 terms. He served as a member of the NACHC board and serves on NACHC committees. He is a regular speaker at the MPCA annual board member training. David currently serves as chair of the MPCA health center board member committee and a member of MPCA Executive Committee. David also is a HRSA approved consultant for technical assistance and site visits.

David has been recognized many times by both NACHC and MPCA for his work with health centers. In addition to his work in the health center community, he is an international bestselling author with multiple books, a keynote speaker and trainer.

69052501R00041

Made in the USA
Columbia, SC
12 August 2019